The Doctrine and Covenants

Come, Follow Me—Activity Book

Arie Van de Graaff

CFI
An Imprint of Cedar Fort, Inc.
Springville, Utah

To the members, missionaries, and investigators of Slovenia
(Doctrine and Covenants 18:15-16)

-Arie

The Doctrine and Covenants

Come, Follow Me—Activity Book

ISBN 13: 978-1-4621-4750-2

Published by CFI, an imprint of Cedar Fort, Inc.
2373 W. 700 S., Suite 100, Springville, UT 84663
Distributed by Cedar Fort, Inc., www.cedarfort.com

Cover design and interior layout by Shawnda T. Craig

Printed in the United States of America

10 9 8 7 6 5 4 3 2 1

Printed on acid-free paper

JOSEPH SMITH SILHOUETTE

In Doctrine and Covenants section 1, Joseph Smith is identified as a weak thing to proclaim the fulness of the gospel. Can you find the one shadow that perfectly matches the picture of Joseph Smith?

THE DOCTRINE AND COVENANTS

Section 1 of the Doctrine and Covenants describes that book as a voice of what? Find out by looking at the box with the objects in it. For each object, count how many are in the picture. Then match the letters from the box with the number of the objects on the lines below.

___ ___ ___ ___ ___ ___ ___

2 5 7 8 6 8 4

ASK OF GOD

Joseph Smith had a spiritual experience when he took a question to God. General conference can be more of a spiritual experience if you'll do the same. Find 10 differences in these pictures.

THE FIRST VISION

In the spring of 1820, 14-year-old Joseph Smith entered a grove of trees near his home in Palmyra, New York and the world was never the same again. See if you can find the hidden objects below.

MORONI VISITS JOSEPH SMITH

Find ten differences between these two pictures of the Angel Moroni's visit to Joseph Smith.

RECEIVING THE PLATES

After several years of visits, the Angel Moroni delivered the golden plates to Joseph Smith.
Find the two images that are exactly the same.

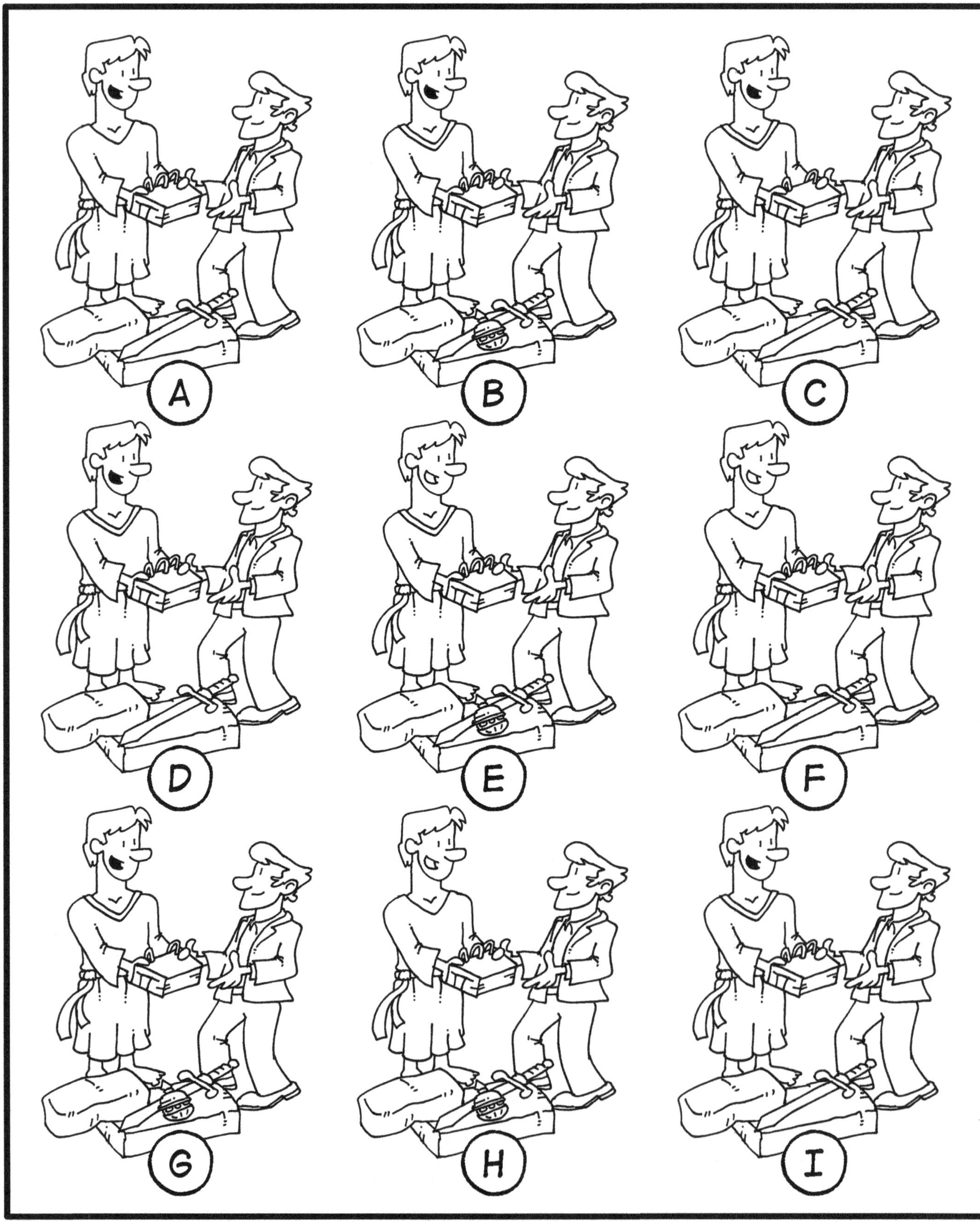

THRUST IN YOUR SICKLE

The Prophet Joseph Smith received an important revelation concerning missionary work directed to his father. Find out which section of the Doctrine and Covenants contains that revelation by identifying the one sickle below that does not have an exact match.

PRINCIPLE OF REVELATION

Which figure of the early Church was taught an important principle of revelation in Doctrine and Covenants 9? Starting out in the upper left hand corner, draw a line from each two-letter bubble that spells out: "Study it out in your mind." The one Church figure not partially crossed out is your answer.

BEHOLD, HERE IS WISDOM

Thousands of years before it happened, the Lord was ready for the lost 116 pages. Find out why Mormon added the small plates of Nephi to the record by matching each square below with the corresponding square in the picture. Record the letter to the left then the top of the squares in the space provided.

P E R W O S

S U A E P I

___ ___ ___ ___ ___ ___ ___ ___ ___ ___ ___ ___

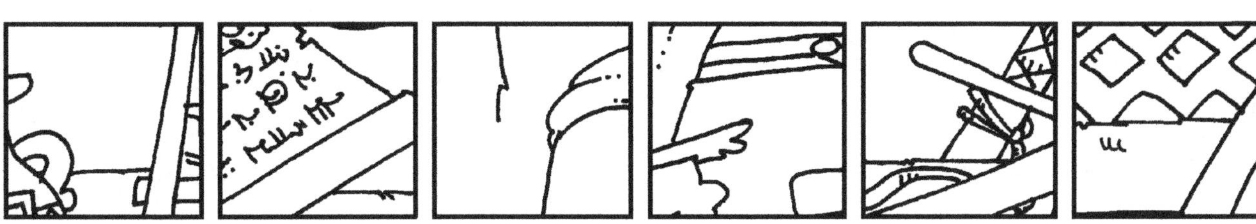

BAPTISM AT THE SUSQUEHANNA

On May 15, 1829, Oliver Cowdery and Joseph Smith baptized each other in the Susquehanna River.
See if you can find the hidden objects in the picture below.

A GATHERING IN THE WOODS

Find out the role the men in this picture played by identifying the object that each man in the picture shares with someone else. Start with Joseph Smith, he's wearing the same suspenders as Hyrum Smith. Now find an object that Hyrum shares with another man in the picture. Record each man's letter as you move from person to person to identify their role.

__ __ __ __ __ __ __ __ __

WORTH OF SOULS

These sister missionaries know that the worth of souls is great in the sight of the Lord. Can you find ten differences between the two pictures below?

LEARN OF ME

In Doctrine and Covenants 19, we learn that Christ's atonement is a great example of an important gospel principle. Find the principle by looking at the box with the objects. For each object, count how many times that object is in the picture. Match the letters from the box with the number of the objects on the lines below.

___ ___ ___ ___ ___ ___ ___ ___ ___

3 7 4 2 1 8 1 4 5

SUNDAY SERVICES

Find out what the most important part of Sunday church meetings is by matching each square below with the corresponding square in the picture. Then write the letter to the left then the letter above those squares in the spaces provided below the picture to find your answer!

THE SONG OF THE RIGHTEOUS

The Lord commanded Emma Smith to prepare a hymnbook for the early saints because "the song of the righteous" is what? Find out by writing the title of each hymn in the set of boxes that match the title's letters. Add each shaded box in order to the spaces below to get your answswer.

Now Let Us Rejoice

O God, the Eternal Father

The Spirit of God

How Firm a Foundation

Adam-ondi-Ahman

Redeemer of Israel

Joy To the World

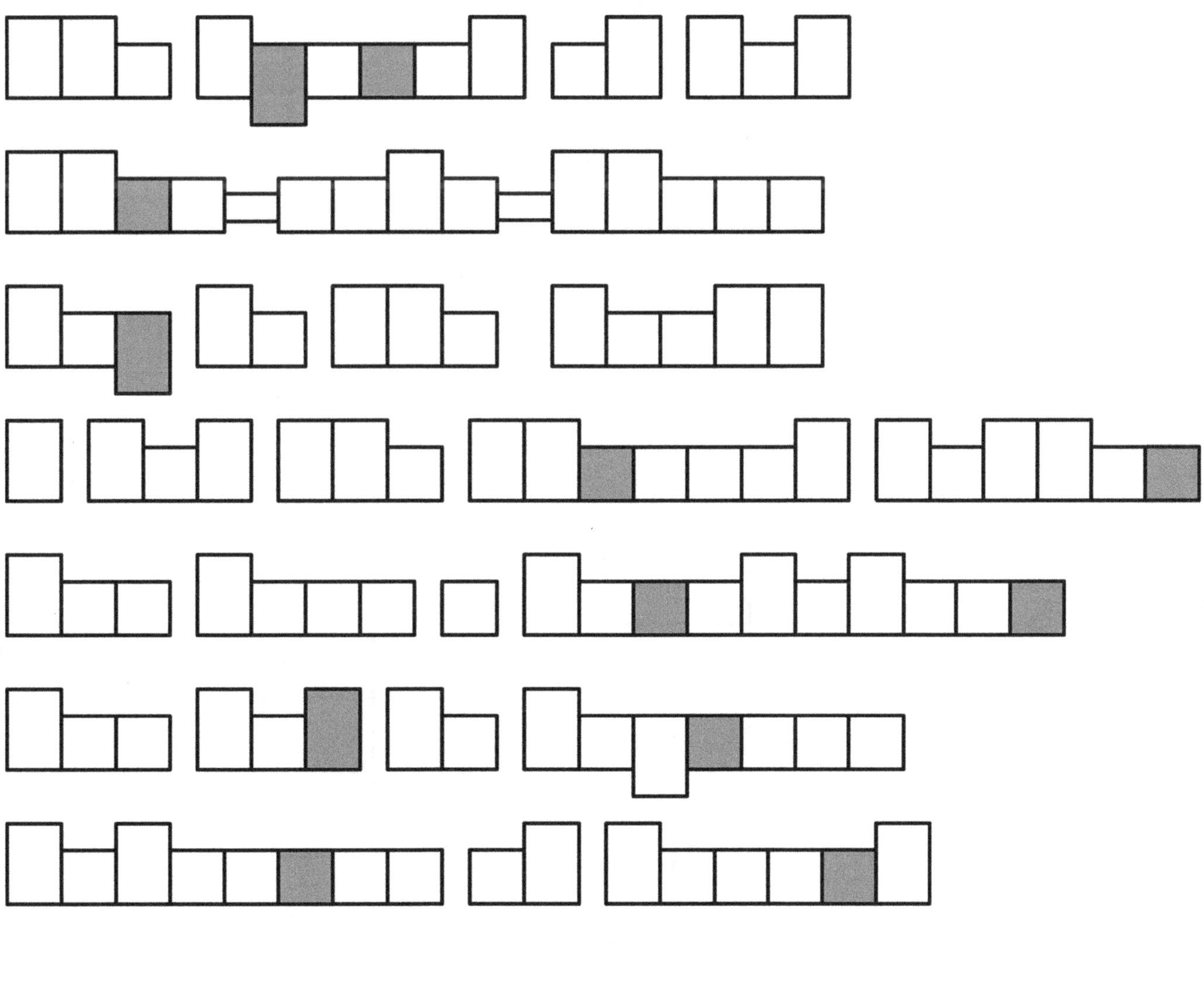

A VERY SPECIAL SACRAMENT MEETING

In Doctrine and Covenants Section 27, the Lord promises Joseph Smith that in the future He will take the sacrament with Joseph and many scripture prophets. Some of those prophets are included below.

Clues:

Abraham	JohnTheBaptist
Adam	Joseph
Elijah	JosephSmith
James	Moroni
John	Peter

Across

1. 2. 3. 4. 5.

Down

1. 2. 3. 4. 5.

JESUS CHRIST WILL GATHER HIS PEOPLE

Doctrine and Covenants 29 teaches that Christ will gather His people. This has been true since the start of the restoration. Can you find five objects that are in each of the pictures of missionaries helping Christ's work? (Bonus: How many apples are on this page?)

CALLED TO PREACH

In the early Church, missionaries were called to preach shortly after their baptisms. Like them, we can share our testimonies with others no matter our age or how long we've been a member of the Church. Can you find the shadow that is the exact match to the picture of the early missionaries below?

EASTER, 1836

On Easter Sunday, 1836, Jesus Christ appeared in a temple to accept the temple as His house. (D&C 110). In which temple did this vision take place? Starting in the upper left hand corner, draw a line from each two-letter bubble that spells out "I am he who liveth." The temple not partially crossed out is your answer.

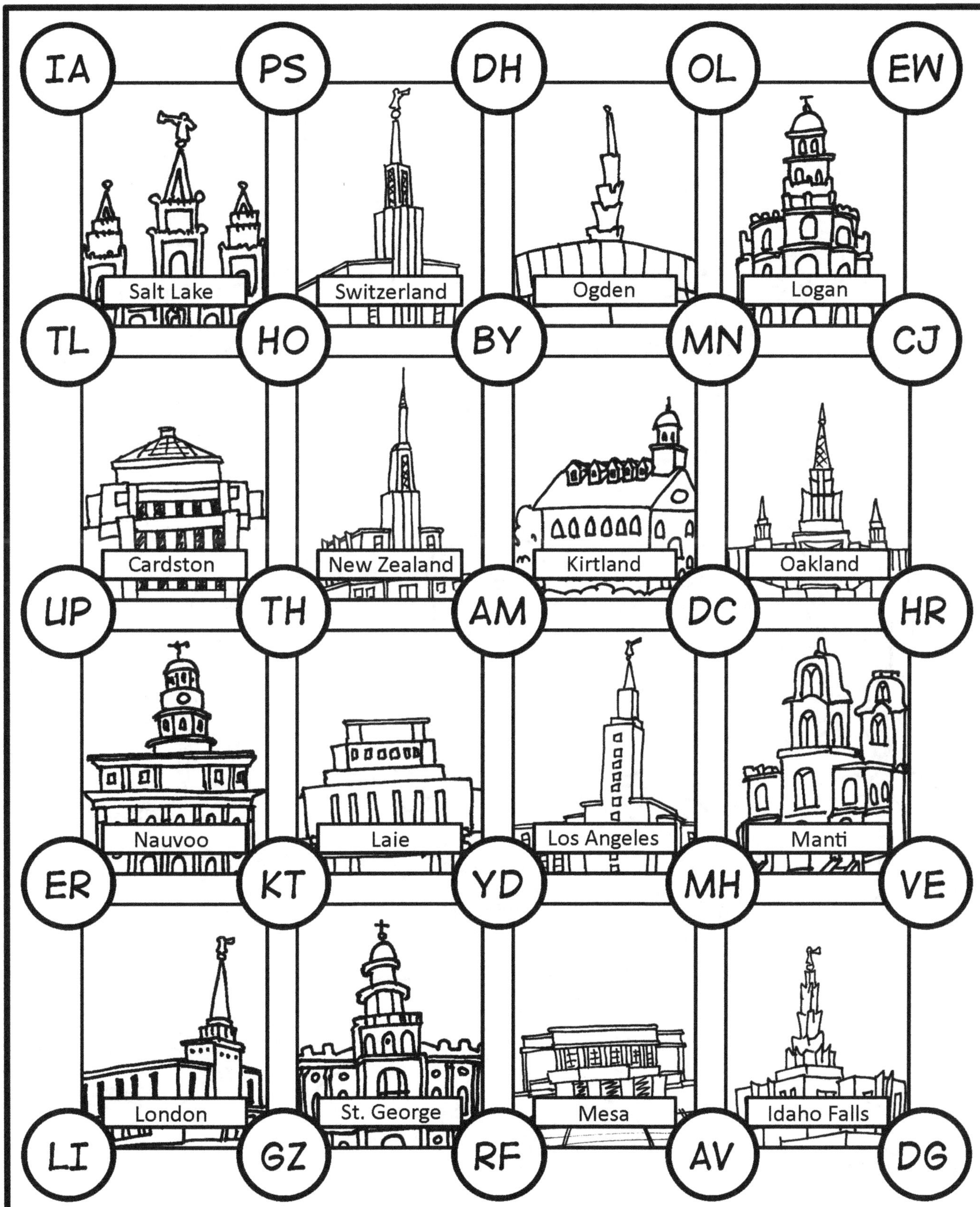

IF YE ARE PREPARED

In January of 1831, the Saints living in New York were commanded to move to Kirtland, Ohio. To comfort these Saints prior to the move, the Lord revealed that “if ye are prepared ye shall not fear” (Doctrine and Covenants 38:30). Find the hidden objects of the Saints packing to move below.

REMEMBER THE POOR

In Doctrine and Covenants 42, we are commanded to "remember the poor, and consecrate of thy properties for their support." Find ten differences between the two pictures below.

STANDARD TO THE WORLD

In Doctrine and Covenants 45, the Lord refers to the gospel covenant as a standard. In ancient times, a standard was a flag used in battle. Find out one role of a standard by crossing out any flags with a matching symbol. Record those that remain below for your answer.

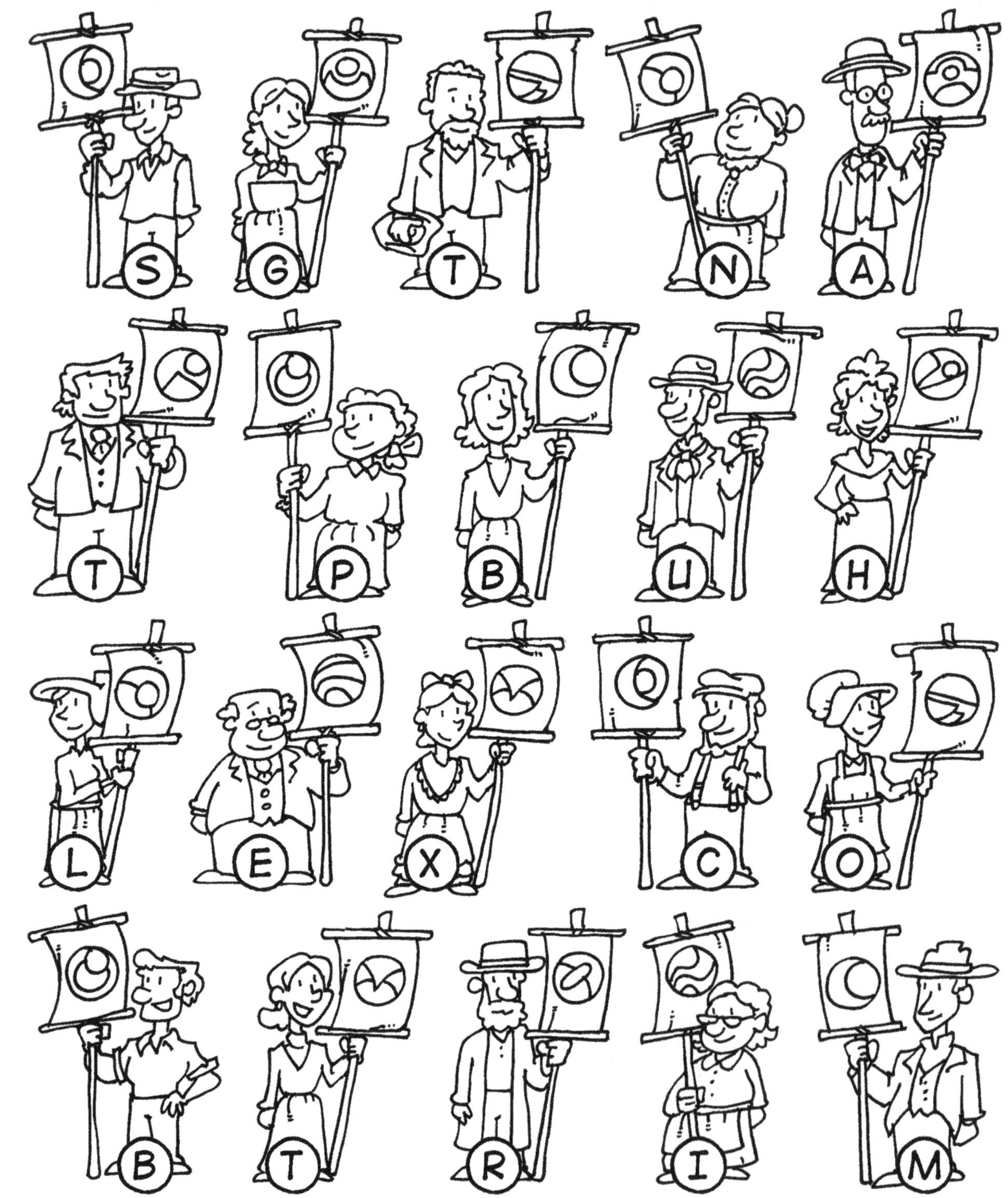

SEEK YE EARNESTLY THE BEST GIFTS

Doctrine and Covenants 46 includes a number of special gifts. Find out where those gifts come from by identifying the matching set of four gifts in the grid with the sets of four gifts at the bottom of the page. Add the letter for each set of four in the empty circles at the bottom to get your answer.

UNDERSTAND ONE ANOTHER

Doctrine and Covenants 50 teaches that if the person teaching and the person hearing both have the spirit, then both of them experience something together. Find out what happens to both the preacher and the receiver when they both have the spirit by matching both ends of the tin cans together.

___ ___ ___ ___ ___ ___ ___

WISE STEWARD

Early Saints practiced the law of consecration where they would sign over their property to the Church. The bishop would then return to you what you needed with instructions to be a wise steward over that which you received. Look over the items on the checklist below. Which three are not inclued in the picture?

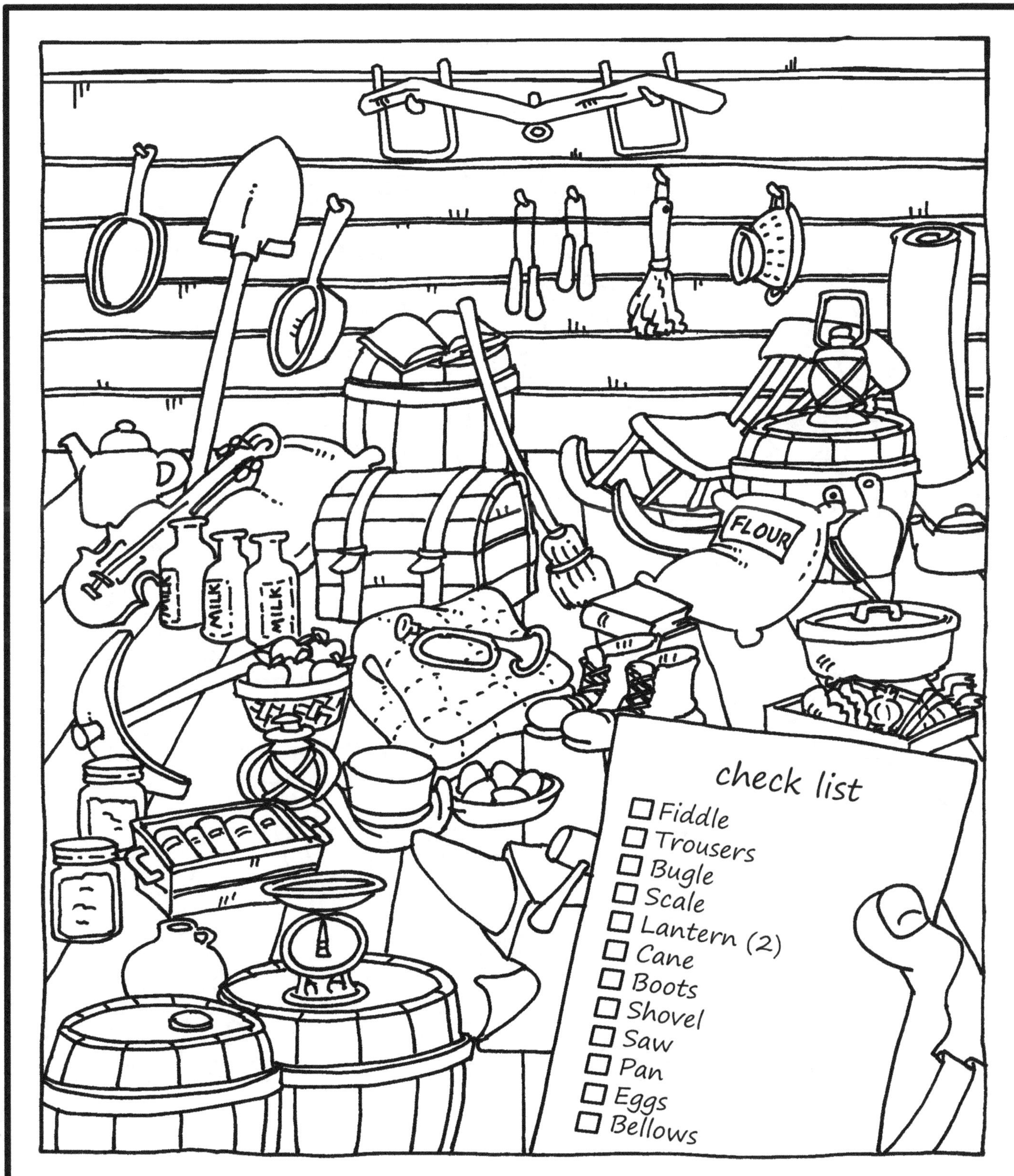

AFTER MUCH TRIBULATION

To the first Saints to arrive in Missouri, Joseph Smith revealed a truth. Find out what comes after much tribulation by identifying the object that each person in the picture shares with someone else. Start with Joseph Smith, he's got the same top hat as the man to his right. Now find an object that man shares with another. Record each person's letter as you move from person to person to find your answer.

___ ___ ___ ___ ___ ___ ___ ___ ___

RIDING THE MISSOURI RIVER

After experiencing a wild day on the Missouri River in his travels from Independence to Kirtland, Joseph Smith received Doctrine and Covenants 61. Find the hidden objects in the picture below.

WELL OF LIVING WATER

In Doctrine and Covenants 63:23, the Lord compares the mysteries of the kingdom to a well of living water. Find the path from the top of the well to the water below.

JOSEPH AND W.W. PHELPS

After an earlier betrayal, Joseph Smith followed the counsel found in D&C 64:10 regarding W. W. Phelps. Find that counsel by matching each square below with the corresponding square in the picture. Record the letter to the left and then the top of the squares in the space provided.

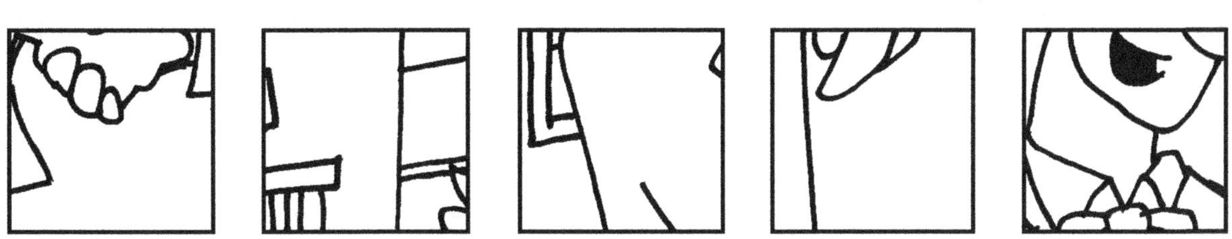

BOOK OF COMMANDMENTS

The first version of the Doctrine and Covenants was called the Book of Commandments. Early Saints considered these scriptures worth more than the riches of the whole what? Find out by crossing out all the riches below that have an exact match. Those that are left will spell out your answer.

BISHOP'S STOREHOUSE

Early bishops like Edward Partridge and Newel K. Whitney were in charge of the bishop's storehouse. Find the hidden objects in this early bishop's storehouse.

THE VISION

Joseph Smith and Sidney Rigdon saw a vision of the eternities that would change the way we understand heaven forever. See if you can find ten changes in these two pictures?

YE CANNOT GO AMISS

In Doctrine and Covenants section 80, we learn that it matters less where you serve than *if* you serve. Find the exact mirror image of the missionaries headed left among the missionaries headed right below.

I AM BOUND WHEN YOU DO WHAT I SAY

At a meeting of high priests and elders, Joseph Smith explained to those present that the Lord is bound to help you when you do what He says. Find the hidden objects below.

MELCHIZEDEK PRIESTHOOD

Sometime in 1829, Peter, James, and John visited Joseph Smith and Oliver Cowdery to restore the Melchizedek Priesthood. Can you find the hidden objects below?

STAND YE IN HOLY PLACES

Doctrine and Covenants 87:8 encourages us to stand in holy places. Start with the Saint in the upper left corner then follow where each Saint is pointing to find the one standing in a holy place.

A HOUSE OF ORDER

Doctrine and Covenants 88 established the School of the Prophets where early Church missionaries could prepare to share the message of the restored gospel throughout the world. Among their direction was to establish a "house of order" for learning. See if you can make order out of the pictures below by finding the two that are exactly the same.

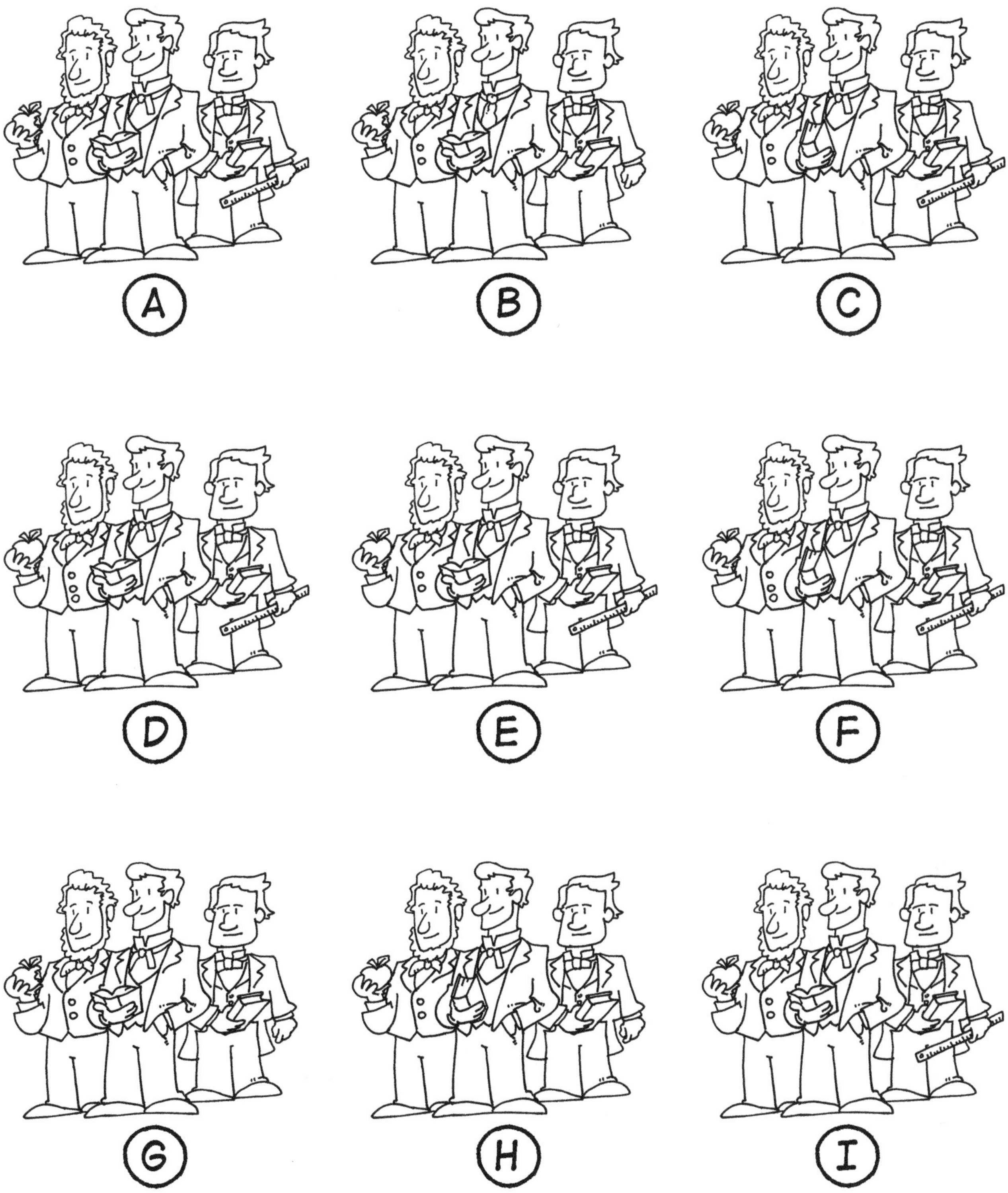

KNOCK AND IT SHALL BE OPENED

In Doctrine and Covenants section 88, the Lord teaches us why we should seek, ask, and knock. Find out what He wants us to do by crossing out any matching doors. Record the letters of those that remain below for your answer.

PRINCIPLE WITH PROMISE

In an upstairs room of the Newel K. Whitney Store, an important commandment was first received. Find out what it was by recording the first letter of each object displayed below.

BRING UP YOUR CHILDREN

Doctrine and Covenants 93:40 directs us to "bring up your children in light and truth."
Can you find ten differences between these pictures of a family studying from the Bible?

THE KIRTLAND TEMPLE

In 1833, construction began on the first temple of the Church. Can you find the hidden objects below?

KNOW THAT I AM GOD

In the midst of terrible persecution in Jackson County, Missouri, the Lord directed His people to "be still and know that I am God." Can you find the perfect reflection between the pictures below?

ZION'S CAMP

After the Saints in Missouri were driven out of their homes in Jackson County, the Lord directed Joseph Smith to organize a company of men to travel 900 miles from Kirtland to assist them. See if you can find the hidden objects below.

SPECIAL GROUP

In February 1835, Brigham Young, Parley Pratt, and Heber Kimball received the same title held by Peter, Paul, and John of ancient times. Find out what by matching each person with his shadow below. Record the letters assigned to them in the space provided.

TEMPLE VISITOR

On April 3, 1836, the Savior Jesus Christ appeared in the Kirtland Temple before Joseph Smith and Oliver Cowdery where He accepted the temple as His house. Find the mirror image of the event below.

COUNSEL FOR THE TWELVE

In Doctrine and Covenants section 112, the Lord offers valuable counsel to the Quorum of the Twelve prior to their missionary service throughout the world. Discover what it is by identifying the object each apostle is holding that he shares with someone else. Start in the upper left corner and work your way through the page. Record each apostle's letter below in order of the objects for your answer.

__ __ __ __ __ __ __ __ __ __ __ __ __

A STANDING LAW

Find out why these Latter-day Saints are planning on giving one of their pigs to the Church. Starting with the pig with a star on its side, move the number of spaces indicated by each arrow while recording the letter of each stop in the spaces provided below.

___ ___ ___ ___ ___ ___ ___

DIGNITY AND MAJESTY

After being arrested and on his way to Liberty Jail, Joseph Smith bravely rebuked a number of guards who were saying horrible things about the struggling Saints in Missouri. Can you identify the two pictures below that are exactly the same?

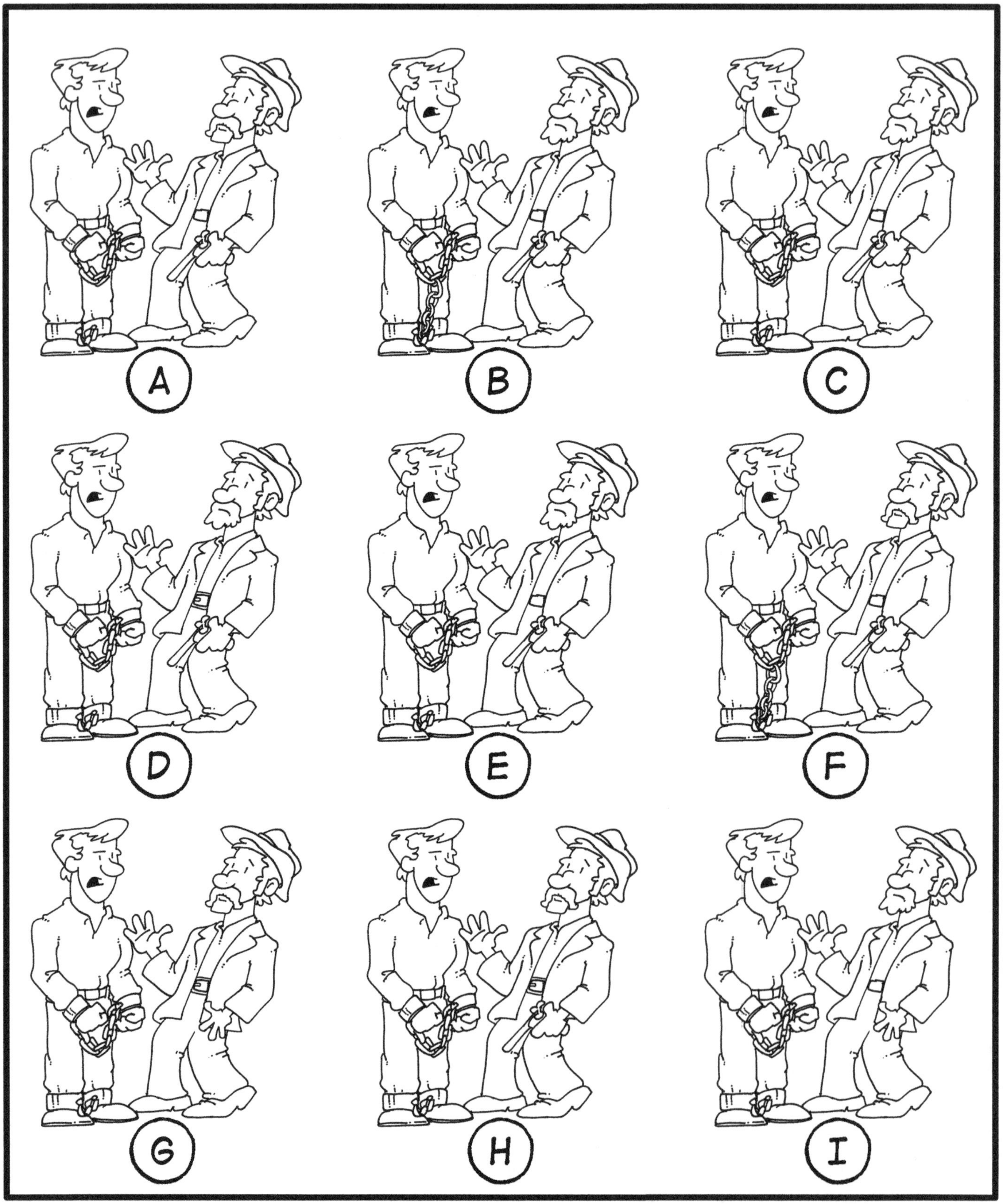

NAUVOO THE BEAUTIFUL

After being forced out of Missouri, the Saints settled and built a beautiful city out of swampland off of the Mississippi River. Can you find all the hidden objects in the picture of Nauvoo below?

RELIEF SOCIETY QUILT

In 1842, the Lord first organized the Relief Society, an organization dedicated to helping others. The Relief Society helps to keep the commandment found in Doctrine and Covenants 124 by providing "health and safety" for all. Identify a major characteristic of the Relief Society by recording the matching set of four quilt squares with the ones at the bottom of the page. Record each set's letter below.

BAPTISM FOR THE DEAD TIC-TAC-TOE

Baptism for the dead allows us to help and connect with our ancestors. We have so much in common with our extended family. Can you find something each set of three family members vertical, horizonal, and diagonal have in common?

ETERNAL MARRIAGE

Joseph Smith taught the exciting doctrine of eternal marriage in Doctrine and Covenants section 131. Find the exact two sets of couples below.

BENEFIT OF MAN

Doctrine and Covenants section 133 teaches that government should be instituted for the benefit of man. Find ten differences in these pictures of U.S. Founding Fathers.

CARTHAGE JAIL

Write the names of the objects that may have been present in Carthage Jail on June 27, 1844. Then match the numbered letters below to identify a title we can give to Joseph or Hyrum Smith.

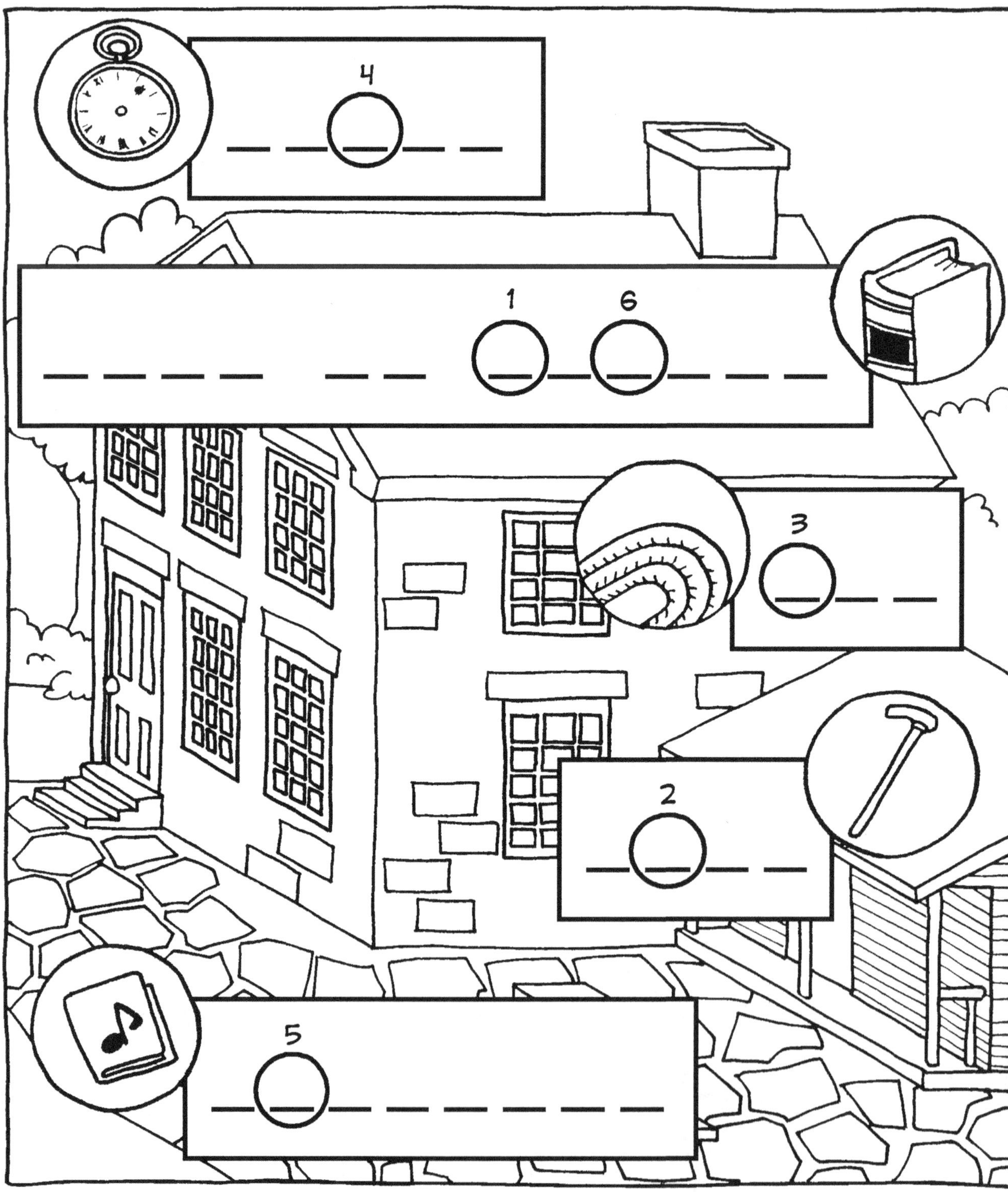

___ ___ ___ ___ ___ ___
1 2 3 4 5 6

MIXED-UP TREK WEST

These pioneers are traveling to the Salt Lake Valley, but there are a number of things about this picture that just aren't quite right. How many things can you find that don't belong?

REDEMPTION OF THE DEAD

Section 138 is a rare section of the Doctrine and Covenants that didn't come from Joseph Smith. Find out which prophet received that revelation regarding the redemption of the dead by solving the puzzle below. Starting in the upper left corner, draw a line from each two-letter bubble that spells out "The eyes of my understanding were opened." The prophet not partially crossed out is your answer.

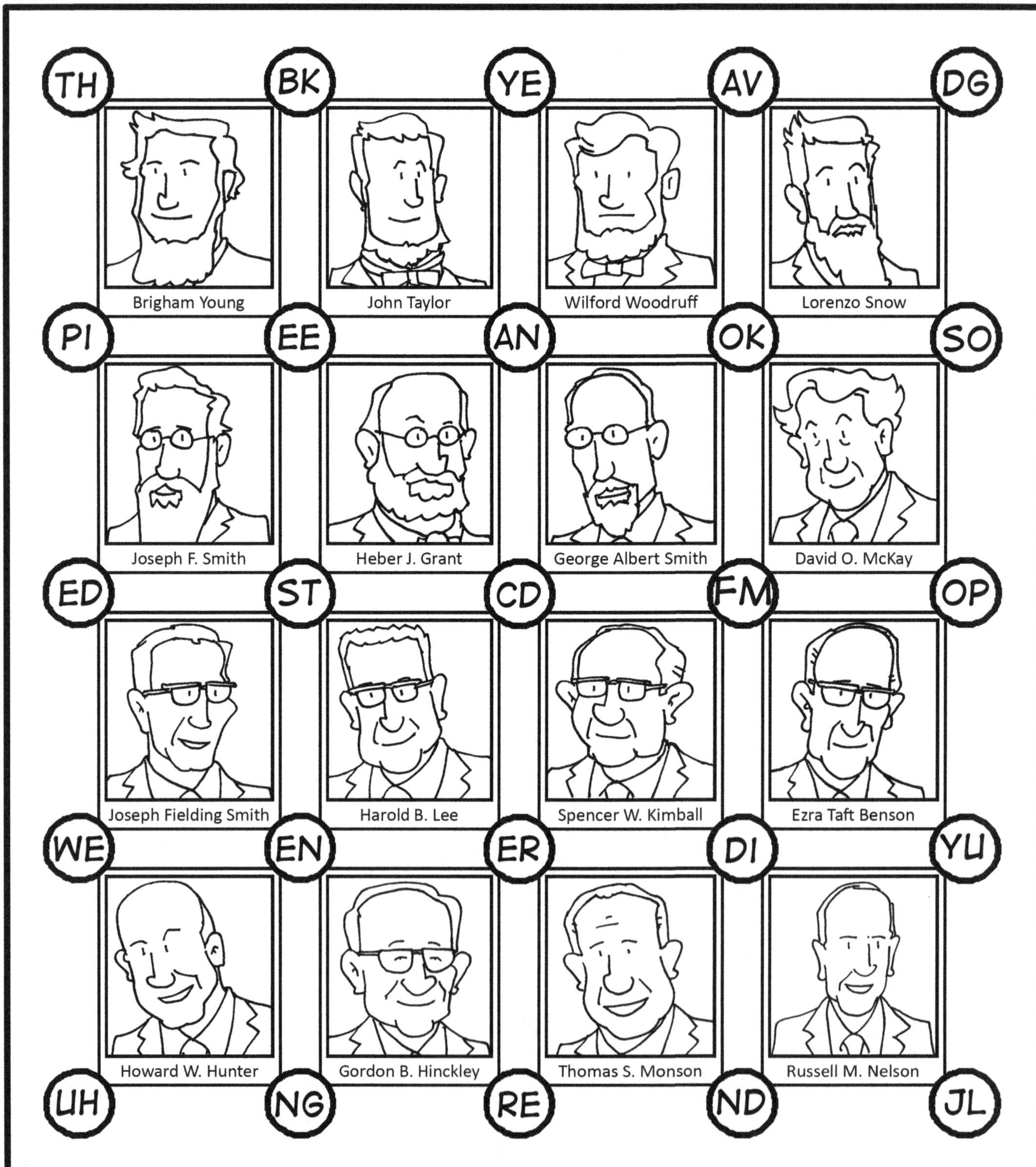

EVERY BLESSING THAT FLOWS THEREFROM

In 1978, President Spencer W. Kimball received the long prayed for revelation that allowed all worthy members to enjoy all the blessings of the priesthood--including the temple. Find the hidden objects in the picture below.

THE PROCLAMATION

The Family Proclamation encourages wholesome recreational activities. Record the first letter of each numbered animal in the spaces below to find out what those activities give to families.

___ ___ ___ ___ ___ ___ ___ ___

1 2 3 4 5 6 7 8

HOLY FAMILY

At Christmas, we celebrate the birth of Jesus Christ. Can you find the two images of Mary, Joseph, and baby Jesus that are exactly the same below?

A

B

C

D

E

F

G

H

I

REASON FOR THE SEASON

Find out why this family is celebrating by looking at the box with the objects in it. For each object, count how many are in the picture. Then match the letters from the box with number of the objects on the lines below.

__ __ __ __ __ __   __ __ __ __ __

4 5 2 3 1 6   4 5 3 11 10

ANSWERS

page 1
B

page 2
Warning

page 3
Bookmark, Bowl, Bucket, Candle (2), Fork, Log, Plate, Mug, Suspenders

page 4

page 5
Ceiling Beam, Clothes on Chair, Headboard, Lantern, Mouth, Quilt Square, Robe, Rug, Sash, Window

page 6
D and I

page 7
Section 4

page 8
Oliver Cowdery

page 9
A Wise Purpose

page 10

page 11
Witnesses

page 12
Book, Cat, Flower Picture, Lamp, Mouth, Mug, Necklace, Picture Frame, Plant, Satchel

page 13
Sacrifice

page 14
The Sacrament

page 15
Prayer Unto Me

page 16
Across: 1. Elijah, 2. Joseph, 3. Adam, 4. JosephSmith, 5. Abraham.
Down: 1. Moroni, 2. JohnTheBaptist, 3. John, 4. Peter, 5. James.

page 17
Apple, Bird, Book of Mormon, Cane, Dog. There are 10 apples.

page 18
A

page 19
Kirtland

page 20

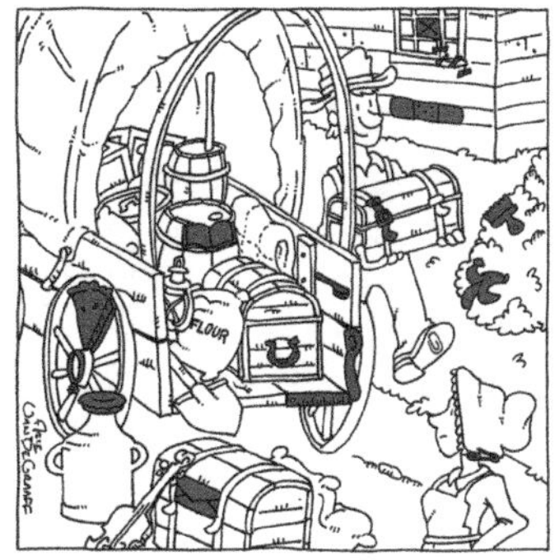

page 21
Apron, Blanket, Bowl, Broom, Candle, Hair Curls, Hat, Picture Frame, Spoon, Suspenders

page 22
Gather

page 23
Spirit

page 24
Edified

page 25
Trousers, Cane, Saw

page 26
Blessings

page 27

page 28

page 29
Forgive All

page 30
Earth

page 31

page 32
Blinds, Bookmark, Eyes, Feathered Quill, Hand, Mirror, Mouth, Paper, Sideburns, Tie

page 33
Bottom Center

page 34

page 35

page 36
18

page 37
E and I

page 38
Draw Near

page 39
Word of Wisdom

page 40
Apron, Broom, Bucket, Buttons, Eyebrow, Glasses, Hair Bow, Mouth, Necklace, Picture Frame

page 41

page 42
Middle Left

page 43

page 44
Apostles

page 45
Bottom Left

page 46
Be Thou Humble

page 47
Tithing

page 48
C and E

page 49

page 50
Charity

page 51
top row: hat, middle row: glasses, bottom row: clock, left column: cactus, middle column: food, right column: water bottle, diagonal down: animal, diagonal up: book

page 52
E and G

page 53
Button, Chair Back, Chair Legs, Feathered Quill, Eyebrow, Hair Bow, Lantern, Picture, Shirt Cuffs, Vase

page 54
Martyr

page 55
At Least 15: Baseball Cap, Dog Driving, Fish Driving, Headphones, Manhole, Palm Tree, Phone, Refrigerator, Roller Skates, Satellite, Skateboard, Sneakers, Stop Light, Sunglasses, Tucana

page 56
Joseph F. Smith

page 57

page 58
Memories

page 59
B and G

page 60
Christ Child